from YES *to* I DO

from YES *to* I DO

an engagement journal

CHRONICLE BOOKS

SAN FRANCISCO

ISBN 978-1-4521-6329-1

Manufactured in China

Design by Hillary Caudle

A Robie Book

10 9 8 7 6 5 4 3 2 1

Chronicle books and gifts are available at
special quantity discounts to corporations,
professional associations, literacy programs, and
other organizations. For details and discount
information, please contact our corporate/
premiums department at corporatesales@
chroniclebooks.com or at 1-800-759-0190.

Chronicle Books LLC
680 Second Street
San Francisco, California 94107
www.chroniclebooks.com

Congratulations! You're getting married!

There is so much excitement and celebration in the months between getting engaged and getting married. And while the proposal and the wedding get a lot of attention, the process of moving from one to the other can be a meaningful transition. It brings up questions about family, love, and togetherness, and involves so many firsts and negotiations with the person you've chosen as your partner in life. Whether you've been thinking about your wedding since childhood or never really gave it a thought, you've been dating for years or had a whirlwind romance, this in-between time is a special moment in your relationship. Sure, there's a lot of planning, but there's so much more that happens in the weeks, months, or even years between saying "Yes" and saying "I Do." And while a wedding planner can capture the name of your venue and the phone number of your caterer, this journal is a place to capture all the thoughts and feelings that will come up over the next few months. Just like a wedding album, this is a place to come back to and remember what it was like at the very beginning of this journey. And unlike an album, these pages can hold all the feelings that can't be seen in a photograph.

There's space on these pages to write down the story of the proposal, good marriage advice and stories you receive along the way, and the memories of wedding preparation before they drift away. But there's also space to think about what marriage and weddings mean to you, record your hopes and dreams for your relationship in the future, and reflect on the things you're excited about for the wedding day. And there's space to note any anxiety, stress, or sadness that comes up during the process, put it down on paper, and then let it go.

The time between getting engaged and tying the knot can be exciting and a little scary, fun and a bit maddening, but the frustration fades while the memories you collect here will last forever. Take note of both the big days that you won't soon forget and the little moments that can easily be lost. This is a space to slow down and savor the commitment you and your love are making to each other. Enjoy every minute of it. And don't forget to look back and remember how your new family started.

the
Proposal

Tell the story of how you got engaged.

Where was it? How did it happen? Were you surprised? Fill in the blanks below and then add the rest of the story. Don't leave out any details so you can really capture the moment and relive it years from now.

After we got engaged, we celebrated by ....,

...., **and** ....

Then we finally told people .... **later.**

....

....

....

....

....

....

....

....

....

....

....

....

The ring.

Some people have one, some people don't,
but there's always a story. Tell yours here.

The Ring

Getting married is about more than just the two of you—

it's about your families coming together as well. Use this space to write about the first time your families met and telling them about the engagement.

....
....
....
....
....
....
....
....
....
....
....
....
....
....
....

The story of how you met.

....

....

....

....

....

....

....

....

....

....

....

....

....

....

What was your first date like?

On finding "The One."

Some people say their sweetheart is "the one" and some think they just found the right person at the right time. When did you know your fiancé was "the one"? Or did you?

....

....

....

....

....

....

....

....

....

....

....

....

....

....

Soon you'll be talking about things that happened during your marriage,

so take a moment to remember some of the best moments and best dates that you've had together so far.

Funniest moments

....

....

....

....

....

....

....

Most awkward moments

....

....

....

....

....

....

Most romantic moments

....

....

....

....

....

....

....

....

Happiest moments

....

....

....

....

....

....

....

....

....

....

Dating doesn't end when you get married,

but you definitely go on more dates in the early part of a relationship. List your favorite dates here, and any inspiration they provide for what you want at your wedding. Plus, it will be great to look back and try to recreate these dates in the future.

THE DATE ....

....

THE INSPIRATION ....

....

....

THE DATE ....

....

THE INSPIRATION ....

....

....

THE DATE ....

....

THE INSPIRATION ....

....

....

At some points during the wedding planning process the going will get a little stressful, but it helps to keep in mind why you're doing this in the first place. List out the things you love most about your fiancé and about your relationship, so you can remember why you're in this together.

My fiancé is the best because

♥ ....

♥ ....

♥ ....

♥ ....

♥ ....

♥ ....

♥ ....

♥ ....

Our relationship is amazing because

♥
....

....

♥
....

....

♥
....

....

♥
....

....

♥
....

....

♥
....

....

♥
....

....

♥
....

What I'm most excited about for the wedding right now

....

....

....

....

....

....

....

....

....

....

....

....

....

....

What I'm most nervous about for the wedding right now

....

....

....

....

....

....

....

....

....

....

....

....

....

....

*These questions will come up several times in the journal. Write down how you feel right now, and once the journal is full, take a look back and remember how you felt during the process.

Congratulations and well-wishes will start rolling in once the news of your engagement is announced.

Some reactions will be sweet, others will be funny, but they're all definitely worth remembering.

....

....

....

....

....

....

....

....

....

....

....

....

....

....

....

....

Take the next few pages to reflect on how you feel about being engaged, about the word *fiancé*, and any other things you want to remember about the proposal. This is the space to capture anything else you're feeling.

....

....

....

....

....

....

....

....

....

....

....

....

....

....

Planning

— for the —

Future

Marriage is a word with lots of weight and meaning to it.

What does it mean to you? Think about what you expect in a marriage, what a good marriage looks like, and what you hope for in a happy marriage. Thinking about it now will provide a good guide for what to strive for in the future and may be a good thing to share with your fiancé once you've organized your thoughts.

It's always good to have some role models in mind.

Think about married couples you admire. Then fill in the blanks to see what they have that you want to strive for.

I admire _____ and _____'s

marriage so much. The way they _____ to

each other, _____ for each other, and

_____ with each other is something I want

to emulate. And the fact that they still _____

after all these years encourages me that my marriage can

_____ as well.

❤ ❤ ❤

_____ and _____ have a

great marriage. Their _____ toward each other,

and the way they _____ is a true testament to

their love. I hope that my fiancé and I can _____

just like they have.

.... and ....—what a great couple. I'm inspired by how they .... together, ... around each other, and .... with other people. Their commitment to ...., ..., and .... each other is something I hope to have in my marriage as well.

♥ ♥ ♥

....

....

....

....

....

....

....

....

....

....

....

....

Many wedding ceremonies include the words "for better or for worse" since all relationships have their challenges.

Undoubtedly, you and your fiancé have had your own challenges in your relationship so far, and will continue to face challenges together in your marriage. Write down some of the challenges you've faced in the past as a reminder of how strong you are. Then write down some challenges you expect to face in your marriage—perhaps related to career, family, children, or where you live—and think about how you plan to face them.

Past Challenges

....
....
....
....
....
....
....
....
....
....
....
....
....
....
....
....
....
....

Future Challenges

....
....
....
....
....
....
....
....
....
....
....
....
....
....
....
....
....
....

When it comes to thinking about the wedding, it can help to have an emotional focus.

Choose from the words below, or come up with your own, and circle or write down five that you want to emphasize in your wedding.

Joy	Big	Creative
Comfort	Small	Handmade
Elegance	Religious	Exotic
Abundance	Casual	Nontraditional
Happiness	Formal	Traditional
Laughter	Unusual	Simple
Meaning	Family-oriented	Luxurious
Intention		Romantic

Now that you have an emotional center, what are your goals for the wedding?

Write down three things that you can come back to during planning to help with decision making. They can be specific, like incorporating loved ones who can't be there into the ceremony, or more general, like making sure everyone feels comfortable.

♥ ....
....
....

♥ ....
....
....

♥ ....
....
....

Time for some imagination.

Write down what your vision for the wedding is in whatever level of detail feels right to you. You might have a lot of thoughts about it, or very few. Regardless, capture your vision here. You can use it as a guide while planning or look back at it when all is said and done and see how your vision changed during the process.

There are many wedding traditions from a variety of cultures that can be used in your ceremony.

Think about weddings you've been to or seen or heard about. What do you love? What do you hate? Write it down so you don't forget.

Love It

Leave It

Every wedding includes vows,

whether they are religious, legal, or handwritten. It's the part of the ceremony that captures the promises you and your fiancé will make to each other and strive to uphold throughout your marriage. Even if you don't plan to write your own vows for the ceremony, it can be meaningful to consider what you personally feel you are promising when you say "I do." What is it that you are committed to providing for this person and hoping to get in return during a lifetime together?

What I'm most excited about for the wedding right now

....
....
....
....
....
....
....
....
....
....
....
....
....
....

What I'm most nervous about for the wedding right now

....

....

....

....

....

....

....

....

....

....

....

....

....

....

....

....

....

Even if nothing went wrong with the wedding planning and your family was perfect, the process of putting together a wedding would still create some stress and anxiety.

It's no surprise if sometimes you feel frustrated or overwhelmed by what's happening. Capture those things that are making you worry, from the big to the small, and then leave them on the page so you can let go and move forward with enjoying your engagement.

These next few pages are a space to capture whatever else you're feeling about the wedding planning process.

Memorable Moments

Moments

— *in the* —

Engagement

The days and weeks of an engagement are made up of small moments (and some big ones) that celebrate your relationship with your fiancé.

This section has space to capture memories from some of those moments as well as space to write down those moments that you want to last forever.

Engagement party memories

....

....

....

....

....

....

....

....

....

....

....

....

....

Bridal shower memories

Bachelorette memories

Rehearsal dinner memories

Other events

The best marriage advice
I received was

The most awkward marriage advice I received was

The sweetest wedding stories that people shared with me were

....

....

....

....

....

....

....

....

....

....

....

....

....

....

Little moments captured.

Check off the ones that have happened to you
and write the date they happened. Then use
the last few lines to write in your own.

♡ **When you chose an officiant**

DATE: ....

DETAILS: ....

....

♡ **When you got your marriage license**

DATE: ....

DETAILS: ....

....

♡ **First time you cried about wedding planning (happy or sad tears)**

DATE: ....

DETAILS: ....

....

....

....

♡ First time you received something addressed to you and your fiancé with one last name

DATE:

DETAILS:

♡ When you received your first wedding RSVP

DATE:

DETAILS:

♡ When you received your first wedding gift and/or card

DATE:

DETAILS:

♡ First time you said, "This is my fiancé"

DATE:

DETAILS:

♡ First time you forgot that you're engaged and then remembered after introducing your fiancé

DATE:

DETAILS:

♡ First time you said, "Forget it, let's just elope"

DATE:

DETAILS:

♡ When you actually just eloped

DATE:

DETAILS:

♡

DATE:

DETAILS:

Choosing the wedding party— or no wedding party.

Deciding on the people who will stand with you on your wedding day is a big decision. It may be that you've always known who it will be, or that you want it to just be you, your fiancé, and the officiant standing at the end of the aisle. Who will be in your wedding party and how did you choose? Tell the story here.

As other moments come up during your engagement, write them down so you won't forget them in the future. Whether funny, sweet, or frustrating, they'll bring a smile to your face when you reflect back on this time.

Just Before

the

Wedding

Imagine your future with your spouse . . .

In one year?

_____

_____

_____

_____

_____

_____

_____

_____

_____

_____

_____

_____

_____

_____

Five years?

Ten years?

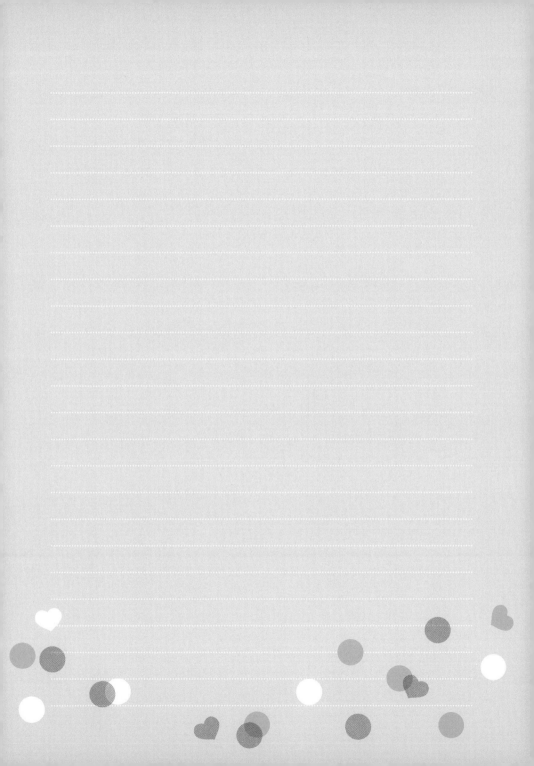

What I'm most excited about for the wedding right now

What I'm most nervous about for the wedding right now

A marriage is the creation of a new family unit.

Regardless of how large that family becomes, it starts with you and your fiancé. While the wedding is the public start of your new family, most couples go into their wedding with traditions of their own that they plan to continue.

What family traditions have you and your fiancé already started and are looking forward to continuing?

....

....

....

....

....

....

....

....

....

....

....

....

What new traditions are you looking forward to starting after your wedding?

_____

_____

_____

_____

_____

_____

_____

_____

_____

_____

_____

_____

_____

No wedding happens without some level of anxiety.

Things happen that are outside of your control, but that doesn't mean those things get to spoil this big moment in your life. Take all the things that are causing stress about the wedding—guests that are driving you crazy, things that you couldn't get done, plans that haven't worked out, or even something like the weather—and get them out on the page. Then let go of those worries so you have space to be truly present on your wedding day.

You and your fiancé have talked about marriage, written vows, made the plans, thought about the future.

How has that changed your vision of what you want in a marriage? What are your expectations about how things will change through the years of your marriage, and what do you hope your marriage will be like?

....

....

....

....

....

....

....

....

....

....

....

....

Some things are hard
to say out loud,

especially when they are full of strong emotions. Use the following pages to write a letter to your future spouse on the week or night before the wedding. Include all the things you want to tell them about how excited you are to start this next step together, how happy you are that they chose you, and how grateful you are to have them in your life.

Dear .... ,

....

....

....

....

....

....

....

....

....

....

....

At this point, all the planning is behind you and your wedding is no longer a vague future thing, but a real event that's happening soon. But the wedding is just one day, and the real work of marriage starts the day after. Take some time to reflect on what you're excited about for the day after the wedding.

Wedding Day Memories

A picture is worth a thousand words,

but a picture can't capture some of the feelings of the day—so this is the place to do it.

What was the weather like?

....

....

How did your wedding clothes feel when you put them on in the morning?

....

....

....

What kind of flowers and decorations did you have? How did they smell? Feel?

....

....

....

What was the cake flavor?

....

....

What was your first dance? And what was the music like for dancing?

....

....

What was your favorite part of the day? Describe it in detail so you won't ever forget.

....

....

....

....

....

....

....

....

....

....

....

....

Everyone says that the wedding day happens so fast that it's hard to remember the details.

The next few pages are a space to recap the events of the wedding and maybe even the days or week leading up to it. Write it down just as it happened so you can relive it again and again through the years.

....

....

....

....

....

....

....

....

....

....

....

....

....

....

A space for gratitude.

A wedding is the work of so many people and part of
the joy is being surrounded by the friends and family
who care about you and your relationship. Many people
supported you and your fiancé during the process of
planning your wedding and throughout your relationship
leading up to this day. Give thanks for them by naming
them and their contributions on these pages.

....

....

....

....

....

....

....

....

....

....

....

....

....

....

What I'm most excited about for my marriage

What I'm most nervous about for my marriage

....

....

....

....

....

....

....

....

....

....

....

....

....

....

The future awaits and only time will reveal how it looks.

But right now, while all the excitement of the wedding is fresh in your mind, write a letter to your future self about your hopes and dreams for your marriage. Wish yourself luck and happiness for your future ahead.

Dear future self,

....

....

....

....

....

....

....

....

....

....

....

....

....

....